Elegant Floral Motifs
Charted Designs

Ursula Michael

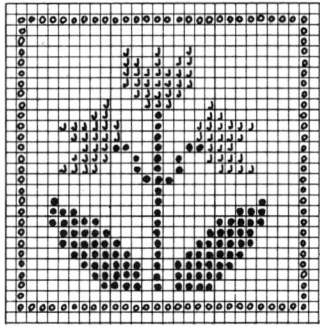

Dover Publications, Inc., *New York*

Models shown on covers were stitched with DMC 6-strand embroidery floss on Charles Craft 14- or 16-count fabric or 28-count Irish linen. The following patterns and products were used:

Front cover (clockwise from top). Rose picture, p. 35; Tulip towel, p. 38, Charles Craft Cross Stitch Estate Towel; Dogwood jewelry box, p. 18, Sudberry House box #99891; Calla box, p. 8, Anne Brinkley Designs box #PLH; Dogwood bookmark, p. 18.

Back cover (left to right). Gentle is the Breath of Spring sampler, p. 46; Campanula tray, p. 11, Sudberry House tray #60138.

Copyright © 1992 by Ursula Michael.
All rights reserved under Pan American and International Copyright Conventions.

Published in Canada by General Publishing Company, Ltd., 30 Lesmill Road, Don Mills, Toronto, Ontario.
Published in the United Kingdom by Constable and Company, Ltd., 3 The Lanchesters, 162–164 Fulham Palace Road, London W6 9ER.

Elegant Floral Motifs Charted Designs is a new work, first published by Dover Publications, Inc., in 1992.

Manufactured in the United States of America
Dover Publications, Inc., 31 East 2nd Street, Mineola, N.Y. 11501

Library of Congress Cataloging-in-Publication Data

Michael, Ursula.
  Elegant floral motifs charted designs / Ursula Michael.
      p.   cm. — (Dover needlework series)
  ISBN 0-486-27079-3
    1. Needlework—Patterns.   2. Decoration and ornament—Plant forms.   I. Title.   II. Series.
TT753.M53   1992
  746.44′041—dc20   91-37948
                                                         CIP

Introduction

Flowers are always a popular design motif for needle-workers, and this collection is particularly appealing. One of its most attractive features is the fact that you can mix and match the designs to create your own "bouquet."

To give you maximum flexibility, each motif is charted on 10-to-the-inch graph paper and is designed to fit within a grid that is a multiple of 10 stitches by 10 stitches. You can easily pick a central motif from one page and surround it with a border from another or create an original sampler like the one on page 46.

To help you plan your design, a blank grid is provided on page 47. Place a sheet of tracing paper over this grid and trace the bold lines that occur every 10 spaces both horizontally and vertically. Choosing various patterns from the book, sketch in the outline of the desired motifs, fitting them into the squares like a puzzle. When your sketch is complete, either transfer the design to a blank 10 × 10 grid or stitch directly from the charts in the book, following the sketch for placement.

To make it easier to combine the motifs, the same color key has been used throughout the book. Rather than referring to actual color numbers, this key has been kept general, since the actual colors you will use will depend to a large extent on which designs you combine.

These designs are perfect for use on pictures, pillows, guest towels, small boxes, bookmarks and the like. A few of the possibilities are shown on the covers of this book.

Although these designs were originally created for counted cross-stitch, they are easily translated into other needle-work techniques. Keep in mind that the finished piece will not be the same size as the charted design unless you are working on fabric or canvas with the same number of threads per inch as the chart has squares per inch. With knitting and crocheting, the size will vary according to the number of stitches per inch.

COUNTED CROSS-STITCH

MATERIALS

1. **Needles.** A small blunt tapestry needle, No. 24 or No. 26.

2. **Fabric.** Evenweave linen, cotton, wool or synthetic fabrics all work well. The most popular fabrics are aida cloth, linen and hardanger cloth. Cotton aida is most commonly available in 18 threads-per-inch, 14 threads-per-inch and 11 threads-per-inch (14-count is the most popular size). Evenweave linen comes in a variety of threads-per-inch. To work cross-stitch on linen involves a slightly different tech-nique (see page 4). Thirty thread-per-inch linen will result in a stitch about the same size as 14-count aida. Hardanger cloth has 22 threads to the inch and is available in cotton or linen. The amount of fabric needed depends on the size of the cross-stitch design. To determine yardage, divide the number of stitches in the design by the thread-count of the fabric. For example: If a design 112 squares wide by 140 squares deep is worked on a 14-count fabric, divide 112 by 14 (= 8), and 140 by 14 (= 10). The design will measure 8″ × 10″. The same design worked on 22-count fabric measures about 5″ × 6½″. When cutting the fabric, be sure to allow at least 2″ of blank fabric all around the design for finishing.

3. **Threads and Yarns.** Six-strand embroidery floss, crewel wool, Danish Flower Thread, pearl cotton or metallic threads all work well for cross-stitch.

4. **Embroidery Hoop.** A wooden or plastic 4″, 5″ or 6″ round or oval hoop with a screw-type tension adjuster works best for cross-stitch.

5. **Scissors.** A pair of sharp embroidery scissors is essential to all embroidery.

PREPARING TO WORK

To prevent raveling, either whip stitch or machine-stitch the outer edges of the fabric.

Locate the exact center of the chart. Establish the center of the fabric by folding it in half first vertically, then horizontally. The center stitch of the chart falls where the creases of the fabric meet. Mark the fabric center with a basting thread.

It is best to begin cross-stitch at the top of the design. To establish the top, count the squares up from the center of the chart, and the corresponding number of holes up from the center of the fabric.

Place the fabric tautly in the embroidery hoop, for tension makes it easier to push the needle through the holes without piercing the fibers. While working continue to retighten the fabric as necessary.

When working with multiple strands (such as embroidery floss) always separate (strand) the thread before beginning to stitch. This one small step allows for better coverage of the fabric. When you need more than one thread in the needle, use separate strands and do not double the thread. (For example: If you need four strands, use four separated strands.) Thread has a nap (just as fabrics do) and can be felt to be smoother in one direction than the other. Always work with the nap (the smooth side) pointing down.

For 14-count aida and 30-count linen, work with two strands of six-strand floss. For more texture, use more thread; for a flatter look, use less thread.

EMBROIDERY

To begin, fasten the thread with a waste knot and hold a short length of thread on the underside of the work, anchoring it with the first few stitches (*Diagram 1*). When the thread end is securely in place, clip the knot.

DIAGRAM 1
Reverse side of work

To stitch, push the needle up through a hole in the fabric, cross the thread intersection (or square) on a left-to-right diagonal (*Diagram 2*). Half the stitch is now completed.

Next, cross back, right to left, forming an X (*Diagram 3*).

DIAGRAM 2

Work all the same color stitches on one row, then cross back, completing the X's (*Diagram 4*).

DIAGRAM 3

DIAGRAM 4

Some needleworkers prefer to cross each stitch as they come to it. This method also works, but be sure all of the top stitches are slanted in the same direction. Isolated stitches must be crossed as they are worked. Vertical stitches are crossed as shown in *Diagram 5*.

DIAGRAM 5

At the top, work horizontal rows of a single color, left to right. This method allows you to go from an unoccupied space to an occupied space (working from an empty hole to a filled one), making ruffling of the floss less likely. Holes are used more than once, and all stitches "hold hands" unless a space is indicated on the chart. Hold the work upright throughout (do not turn as with many needlepoint stitches).

When carrying the thread from one area to another, run the needle under a few stitches on the wrong side. Do not carry thread across an open expanse of fabric as it will be visible from the front when the project is completed.

To end a color, weave in and out of the underside of the stitches, making a scallop stitch or two for extra security (*Diagram 6*). When possible, end in the same direction in which you were working, jumping up a row if necessary (*Diagram 7*). This prevents holes caused by stitches being pulled in two directions. Trim the thread ends closely and do not leave any tails or knots as they will show through the fabric when the work is completed.

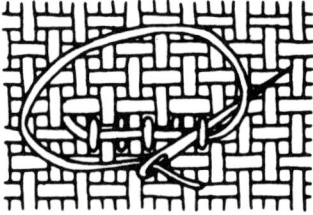

DIAGRAM 6
Reverse side of work

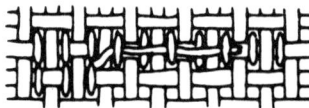

DIAGRAM 7
Reverse side of work

A number of other counted-thread stitches can be used in cross-stitch. Backstitch (*Diagram 8*) is used for outlines, face details and the like. It is worked from hole to hole, and may be stitched as a vertical, horizontal or diagonal line.

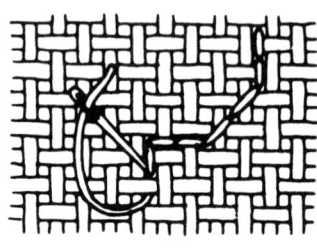

DIAGRAM 8

Straight stitch is worked from side to side over several threads (*Diagram 9*) and affords solid coverage.

DIAGRAM 9

French knots (*Diagram 10*) are handy for special effects. They are worked in the same manner as on regular embroidery.

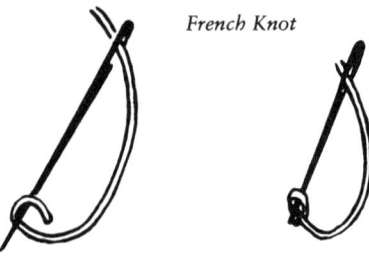

French Knot

DIAGRAM 10

Embroidery on Linen. Working on linen requires a slightly different technique. While evenweave linen is remarkably regular, there are always a few thick or thin threads. To keep the stitches even, cross-stitch is worked over two threads in each direction (*Diagram 11*).

DIAGRAM 11

As you are working over more threads, linen affords a greater variation in stitches. A half-stitch can slant in either direction and is uncrossed. A three-quarters stitch is shown in *Diagram 12*.

DIAGRAM 12

Diagram 13 shows the backstitch worked on linen.

DIAGRAM 13

Embroidery on Gingham. Gingham and other checked fabrics can be used for cross-stitch. Using the fabric as a guide, work the stitches from corner to corner of each check.

Embroidery on Uneven-Weave Fabrics. If you wish to work cross-stitch on an uneven-weave fabric, baste a lightweight Penelope needlepoint canvas to the material. The design can then be stitched by working the cross-stitch over the double mesh of the canvas. When working in this manner, take care not to catch the threads of the canvas in the embroidery. After the cross-stitch is completed, remove the basting threads. With tweezers remove first the vertical threads, one strand at a time, of the needlepoint canvas, then the horizontal threads.

NEEDLEPOINT

One of the most common methods for working needlepoint is from a charted design. By simply viewing each square of a chart as a stitch on the canvas, the patterns quickly and easily translate from one technique to another.

MATERIALS

1. **Needles.** A blunt tapestry needle with a rounded tip and an elongated eye. The needle must clear the hole of the canvas without spreading the threads. For No. 10 canvas, a No. 18 needle works best.

2. **Canvas.** There are two distinct types of needlepoint canvas: single-mesh (mono canvas) and double-mesh (Penelope canvas). Single-mesh canvas, the more common of the two, is easier on the eyes as the spaces are slightly larger. Double-mesh canvas has two horizontal and two vertical threads forming each mesh. The latter is a very stable canvas on which the threads stay securely in place as the work progresses. Canvas is available in many sizes, from 5 mesh-per-inch to 18 mesh-per-inch, and even smaller. The number of mesh-per-inch will, of course, determine the dimensions of the finished needlepoint project. A 60 square × 120 square chart will measure 12″ × 24″ on 5 mesh-to-the-inch canvas, 5″ × 10″ on 12 mesh-to-the-inch canvas. The most common canvas size is 10 to the inch.

3. **Yarns.** Persian, crewel and tapestry yarns all work well on needlepoint canvas.

PREPARING TO WORK

Allow 1″ to 1½″ blank canvas all around. Bind the raw edges of the canvas with masking tape or machine-stitched double-fold bias tape.

There are few hard-and-fast rules on where to begin the design. It is best to complete the main motif, then fill in the background as the last step.

For any guidelines you wish to draw on the canvas, take care that your marking medium is waterproof. Nonsoluble inks, acrylic paints thinned with water so as not to clog the mesh, and waterproof felt-tip pens all work well. If unsure, experiment on a scrap of canvas.

When working with multiple strands (such as Persian yarn) always separate (strand) the yarn before beginning to stitch. This one small step allows for better coverage of the canvas. When you need more than one piece of yarn in the needle, use separate strands and do not double the yarn. For example: If you need two strands of 3-ply Persian yarn, use two separated strands. Yarn has a nap (just as fabrics do) and can be felt to be smoother in one direction than the other. Always work with the nap (the smooth side) pointing down.

For 5 mesh-to-the-inch canvas, use six strands of 3-ply yarn; for 10 mesh-to-the-inch canvas, use three strands of 3-ply yarn.

STITCHING

Cut yarn lengths 18″ long. Begin needlepoint by holding about 1″ of loose yarn on the wrong side of the work and working the first several stitches over the loose end to secure it. To end a piece of yarn, run it under several completed stitches on the wrong side of the work.

There are hundreds of needlepoint stitch variations, but tent stitch is universally considered to be *the* needlepoint stitch. The most familiar versions of tent stitch are half-cross stitch, continental stitch and basket-weave stitch.

Half-cross stitch (*Diagram 14*) is worked from left to right. The canvas is then turned around and the return row is again stitched from left to right. Holding the needle vertically, bring it to the front of the canvas

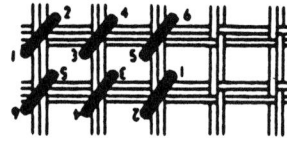

DIAGRAM 14

through the hole that will be the bottom of the first stitch. Keep the stitches loose for minimum distortion and good coverage. Half-cross stitch is best worked on a double-mesh canvas.

Continental stitch (*Diagram 15*) begins in the upper right-hand corner and is worked from right to left. The needle is slanted and always brought out a mesh ahead. The resulting stitch appears as a half-cross stitch on the front and as a slanting stitch on the back. When the row is complete, turn the canvas around to work the return row, continuing to stitch from right to left.

DIAGRAM 15

Basket-weave stitch (*Diagram 16*) begins in the upper right-hand corner with four continental stitches (two stitches worked horizontally across the top and two placed directly below the first stitch). Work diagonal rows, the first slanting up and across the canvas from right to left, and the next down and across from left to right. Moving down the canvas from left to right, the needle is in a vertical position; working in the opposite direction, the needle is horizontal.

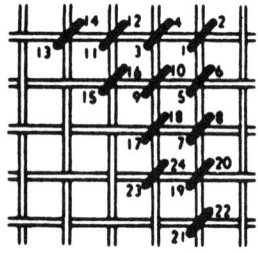

DIAGRAM 16

The rows interlock, creating a basket-weave pattern on the wrong side. If the stitch is not done properly, a faint ridge will show where the pattern was interrupted. On basket-weave stitch, always stop working in the middle of a row,

rather than at the end, so that you will know in which direction you were working.

KNITTING

Charted designs can be worked into stockinette stitch as you are knitting, or they can be embroidered with duplicate stitch when the knitting is complete. For the former, wind the different colors of yarn on bobbins and work in the same manner as in Fair Isle knitting. A few quick Fair Isle tips: (1) Always bring up the new color yarn from under the dropped color to prevent holes. (2) Carry the color not in use loosely across the wrong side of the work, but not more than three or four stitches without twisting the yarns. If a color is not in use for more than seven or eight stitches, it is usually best to drop that color yarn and rejoin a new bobbin when the color is again needed.

CROCHET

There are a number of ways in which charts can be used for crochet. Among them are:

SINGLE CROCHET

Single crochet is often seen worked in multiple colors. When changing colors, always pick up the new color for the last yarn-over of the old color. The color not in use can be carried loosely across the back of the work for a few stitches, or you can work the single crochet over the unused color. The latter method makes for a neater appearance on the wrong side, but sometimes the old color peeks through the stitches. This method can also be applied to half-double crochet and double crochet, but keep in mind that the longer stitches will distort the design.

FILET CROCHET

This technique is nearly always worked from charts and uses only one color thread. The result is a solid-color piece with the design filled in and the background left as an open mesh. Care must be taken in selecting the design, as the longer stitch causes distortion.

AFGHAN CROCHET

The most common method here is cross-stitch worked over the afghan stitch. Complete the afghan crochet project. Then, following the chart for color placement, work cross-stitch over the squares of crochet.

OTHER CHARTED METHODS

Latch hook, Assisi embroidery, beading, cross-stitch on needlepoint canvas (a European favorite) and lace net embroidery are among the other needlework methods worked from charts.

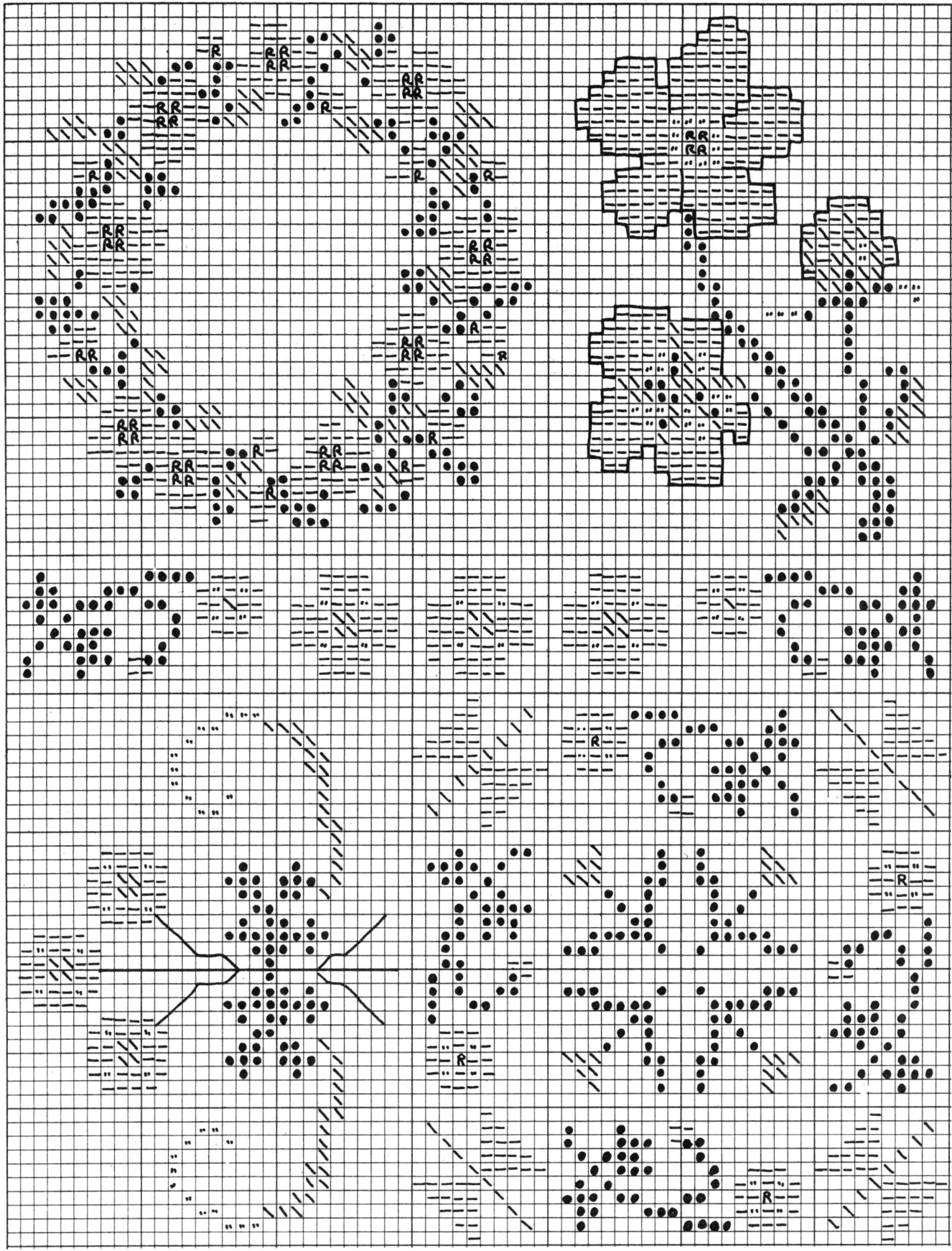

Buttercup

−	yellow	R	yellow green
●	green	−	yellow green backstitch
⟍	light green	••	light brown

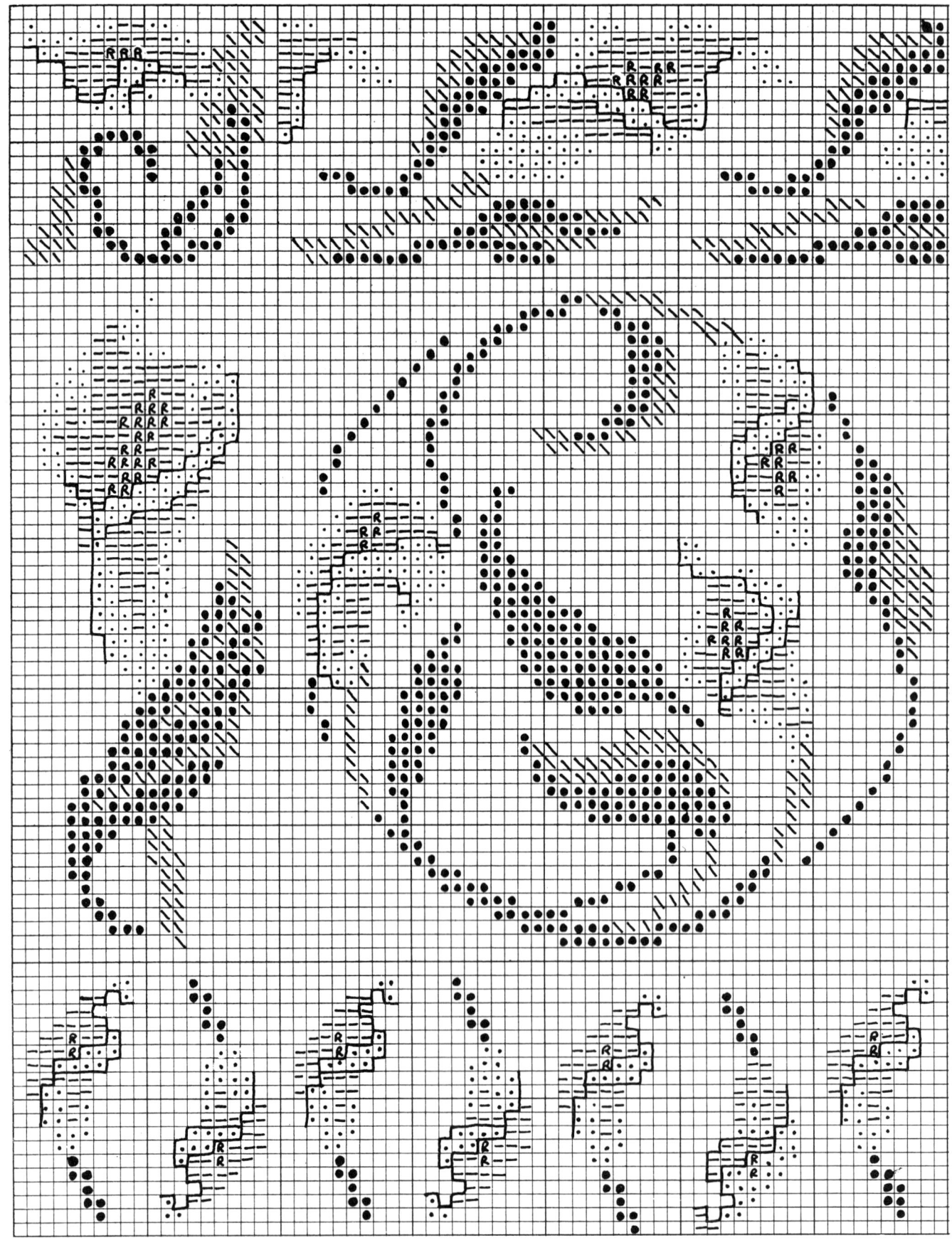

Calla

⊟	yellow	◩ light green
⊡	white	ℝ yellow green
⊙	green	— yellow green backstitch

Clematis

▼ very dark red	· white
⁄⁄ dark red	⅋ gold
✗ dark pink	⟍ light green
c pink	— black backstitch
P light yellow	

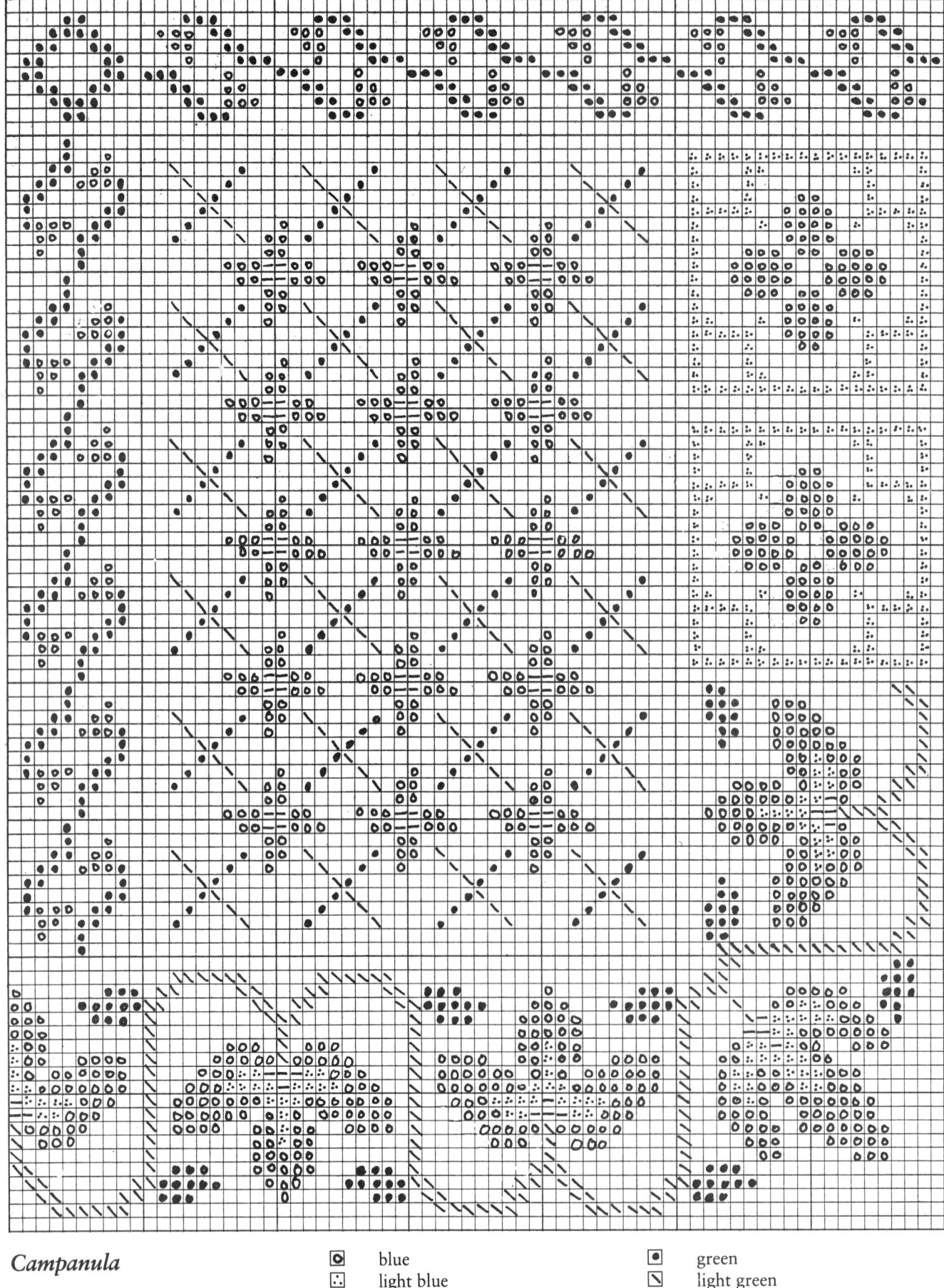

Campanula

⊡ blue		⊙ green
∴ light blue		◣ light green
⊟ yellow		

Campanula

	blue		green
	light blue		light green
	yellow		

Chrysanthemum

—	dark pink backstitch	
c	pink	
–	yellow	

·	green	
··	light brown	

12

Chrysanthemum

☒ dark pink	⊡ green
☐ pink	╲ light green
— gold backstitch	⊡⊡ light brown
⊟ yellow	▨ black
ℙ light yellow	

Chrysanthemum

⊟	yellow	◨	light green
⊠	gold	⊙	blue
⊡	green	⊘	brown

Cornflower

⊡	blue	⊡	green
⧄	light pink	⧅	light green

Crocus

a	violet	◣	light green
v	light violet	⊘	brown
−	yellow	∷	light brown
•	green		

16

Daisy

⊡	white
P	light yellow
⊠	gold
⊙	green

◨	light green
⊘	brown
—	medium gray backstitch

17

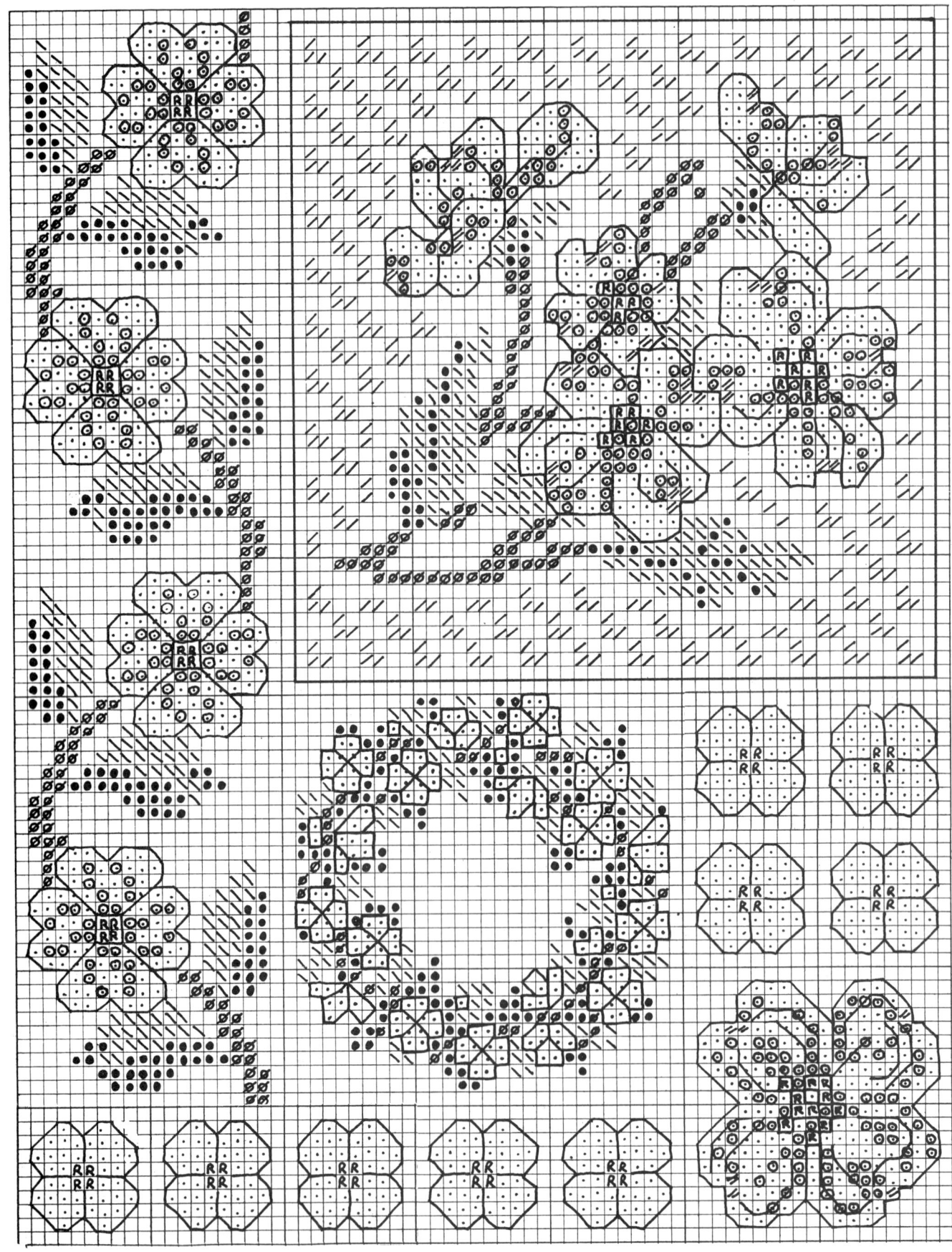

Dogwood

18

⊡ white		⬤ green
⊙ very light pink		◪ light green
⊘ light pink		R yellow green
⊘⊘ dark red		⊘ brown
— dark red backstitch		

Gentian

	blue			green
	light blue			light green

Iris

⊟	dark violet	◥	light green
ⓐ	violet	◼	black
⊙	green		

20

Iris

⊟	dark violet	⊙	green
ⓐ	violet	⧅	light green
ⓡ	gold		

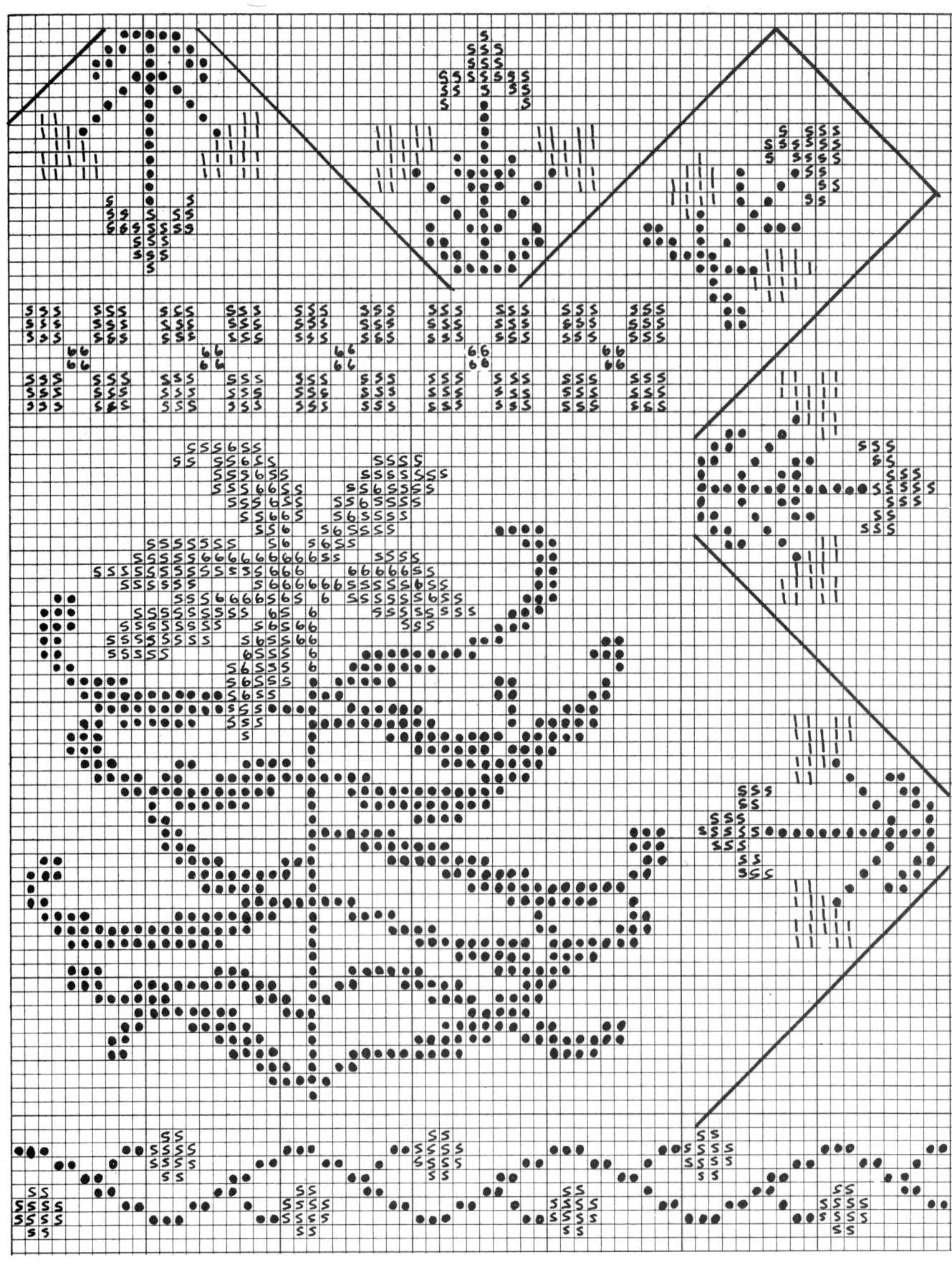

Lily

6	dark peach	**·** green
S	peach	**—** green backstitch
I	light peach	

Lily

6	dark peach
S	peach
1	light peach
●	green

◣	light green
▲	dark brown
—	brown backstitch

Lily

6	dark peach	⦿ green
S	peach	◨ light green
I	light peach	— brown backstitch

Lily of the Valley

⊡	white		◻	light green
⬤	green		—	yellow green backstitch

Mallow

	dark pink		green
☒		◉	
⊆	pink	—	green backstitch
⧄	light pink	◣	light green
☒	dark green	ℙ	light yellow

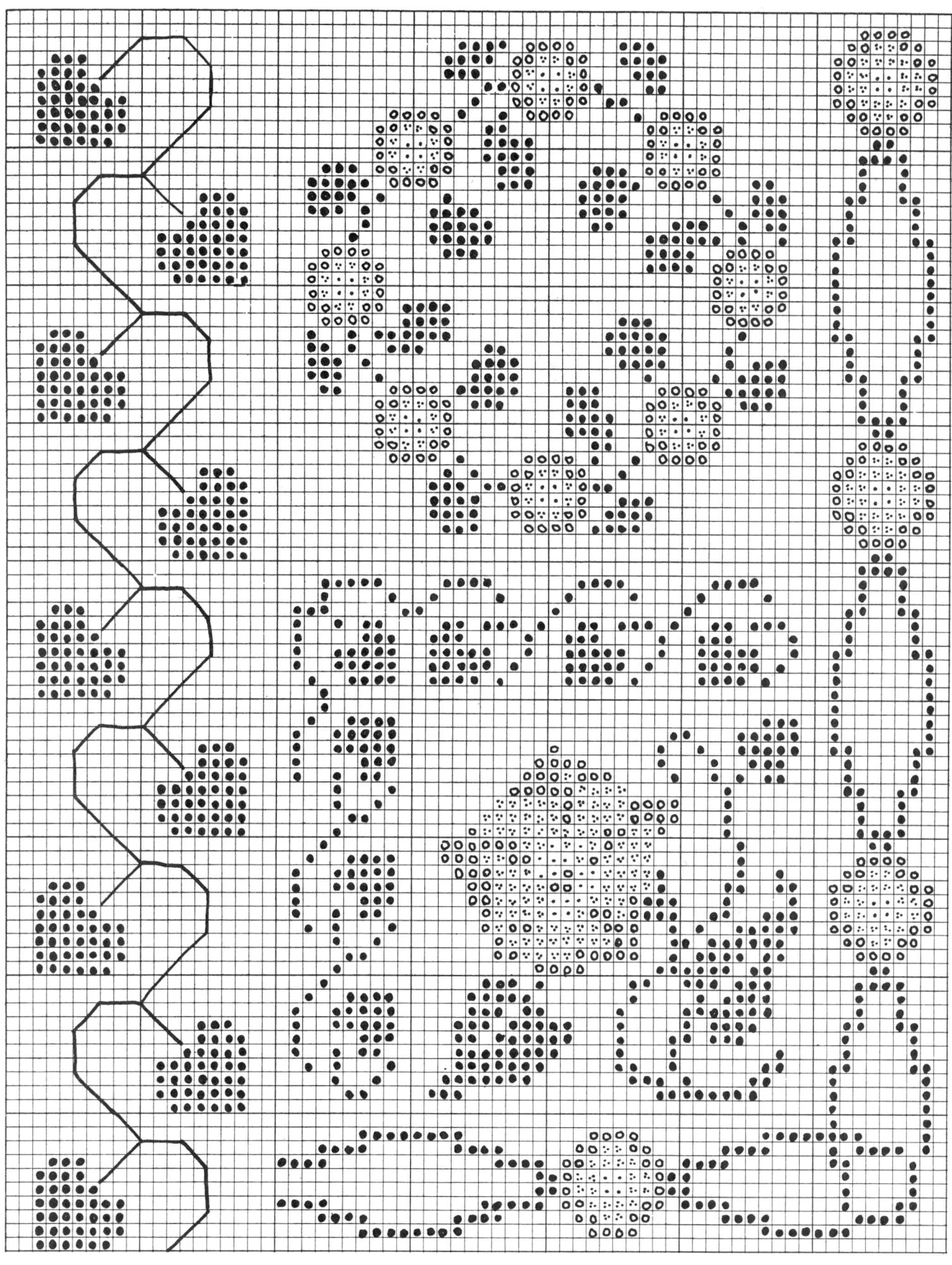

Morning Glory

	blue
	light blue
	white

	green
—	green backstitch

Morning Glory

J	red	⊡	green
☒	light pink	◻	light green
⊡	white	⊡⊡	light brown

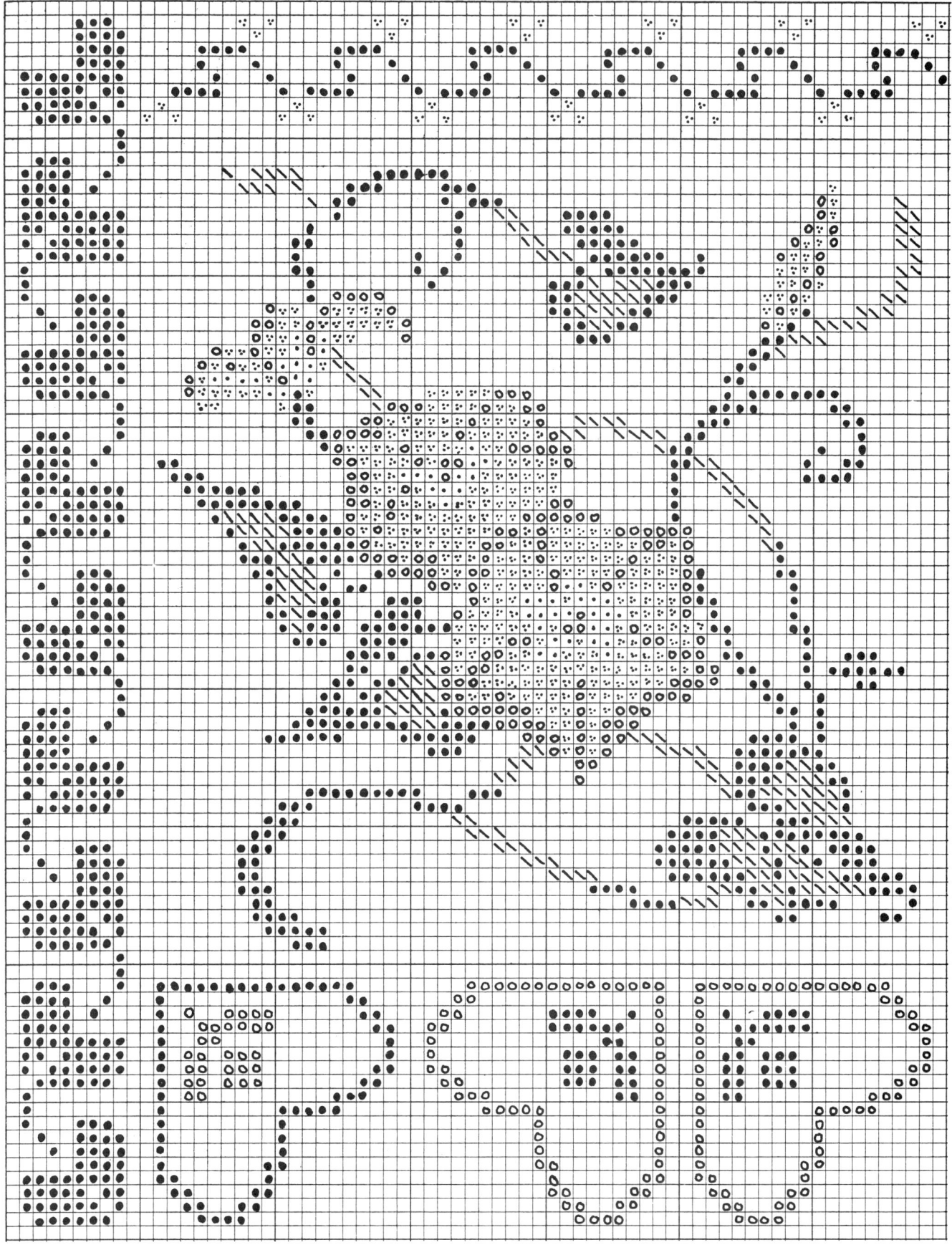

Morning Glory

⊡ blue		⊙ green
⊡ light blue		◨ light green
· white		

Poppy

⟋⟋ dark red	◣ light green	
J red	▣ black	
⦂ light red	— black backstitch	
◉ green		

Poppy

⁄⁄	dark red
J	red
:	light red
–	yellow
Z	dark green
●	green
■	black

Pansy

⊟	dark violet	⊟	yellow
ⓐ	violet	⊠	gold
✚	dark blue	⊡	green
⊙	blue	⧅	light green
⋰	light blue		

Work geometric designs in backstitch using color desired.

Sunflower

⊟	yellow	
⊘	dark red	
⊙	green	
◩	light green	

⧄	brown
—	brown backstitch
⊡	light brown

Rose

C pink		**●** green	
/ light pink		**** light green	
S peach		**••** light brown	

Rose

— very dark pink backstitch	⊡ green
⊠ dark pink	◱ light green
⊂ pink	•• light brown
⧄ light pink	

Rose Borders

☒	dark pink	
☐	pink	● green
☑	light pink	◻ light green

Roses on a Trellis

—	very dark pink backstitch		⊠	gold
⊠	dark pink		·	white
C	pink		●	green
∕	light pink		⊠	light green
⊙	blue		⊘	brown

Tulip

—	dark red backstitch	S	peach
J	red	•	green
∴	light red	◇	light green

38

Tulip

J	red	
X	dark pink	
—	dark pink backstitch	
C	pink	
●	green	

Zinnia

⁄⁄ dark red	⊟ yellow
⑤ peach	⦿ green

Blue Flowers

⊞ dark blue		⊟ yellow
⊡ blue		⦿ green
⸬ light blue		◥ light green

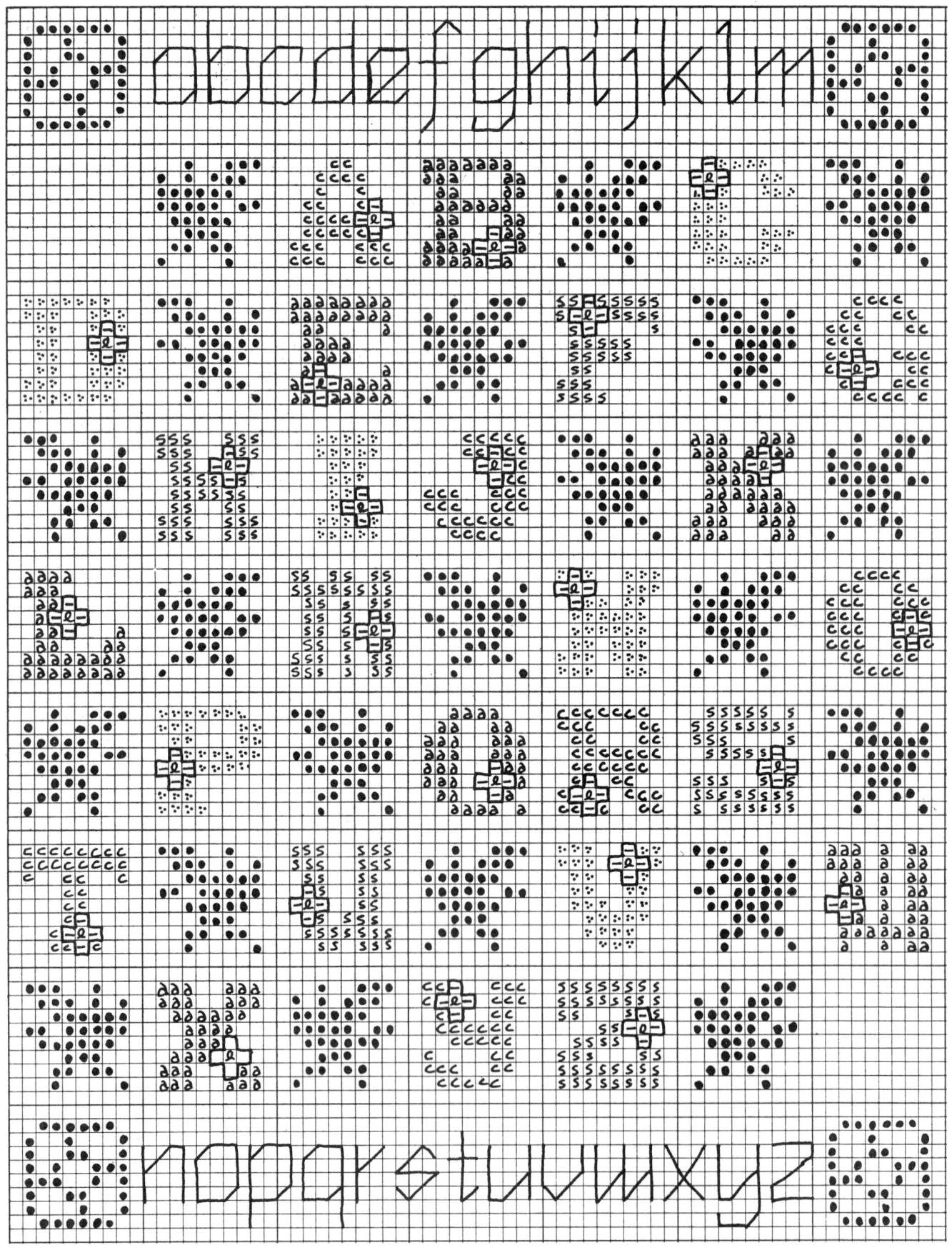

Alphabet

—	dark red backstitch	
⊠	gold	
⊟	yellow	
∴	light blue	
ⓐ	violet	
ⓒ	pink	
ⓢ	peach	
●	green	

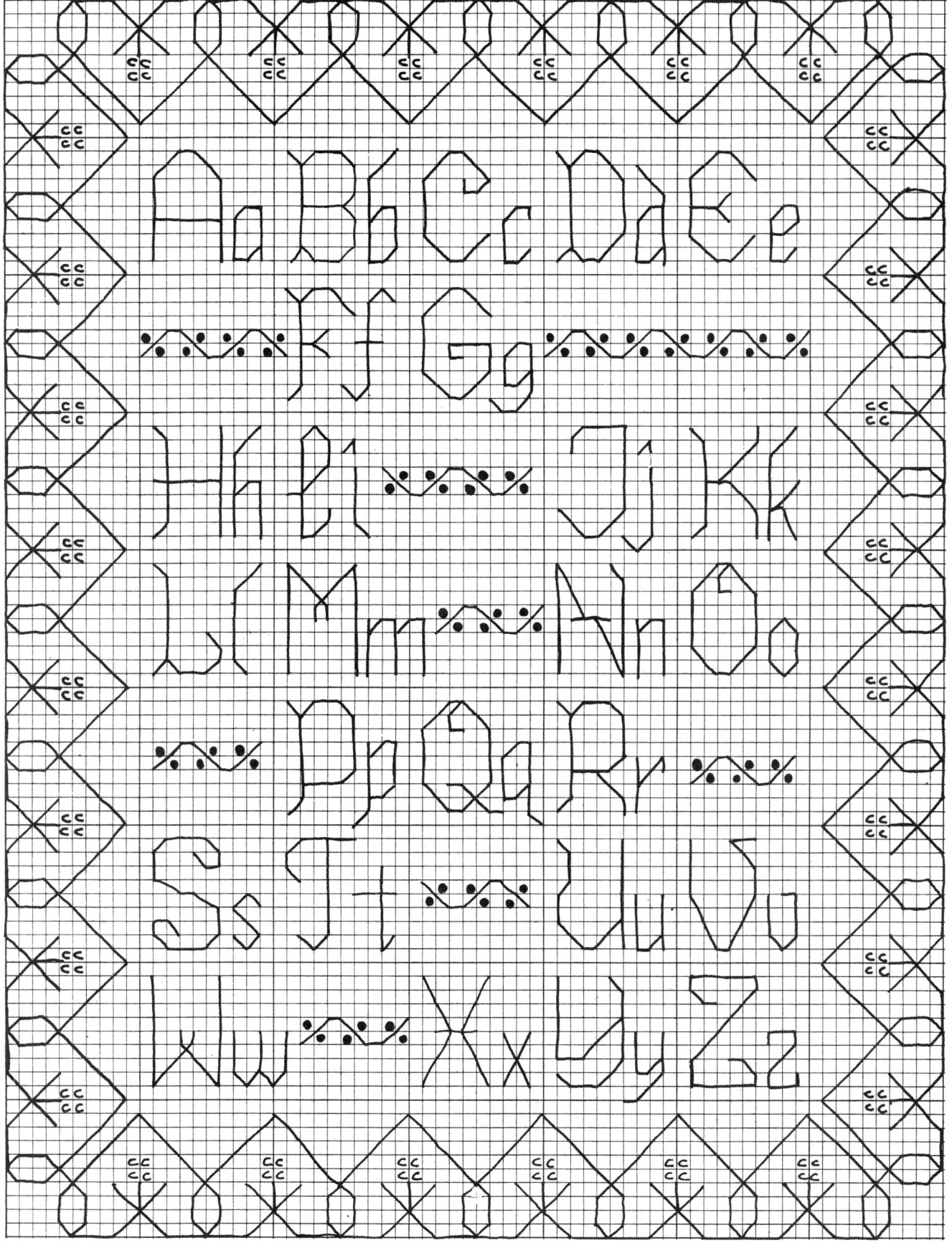

Alphabet

ⓒ   pink

▣   green

Heavy lines indicate backstitch. Work letters in blue, hearts in dark red and vines in green.

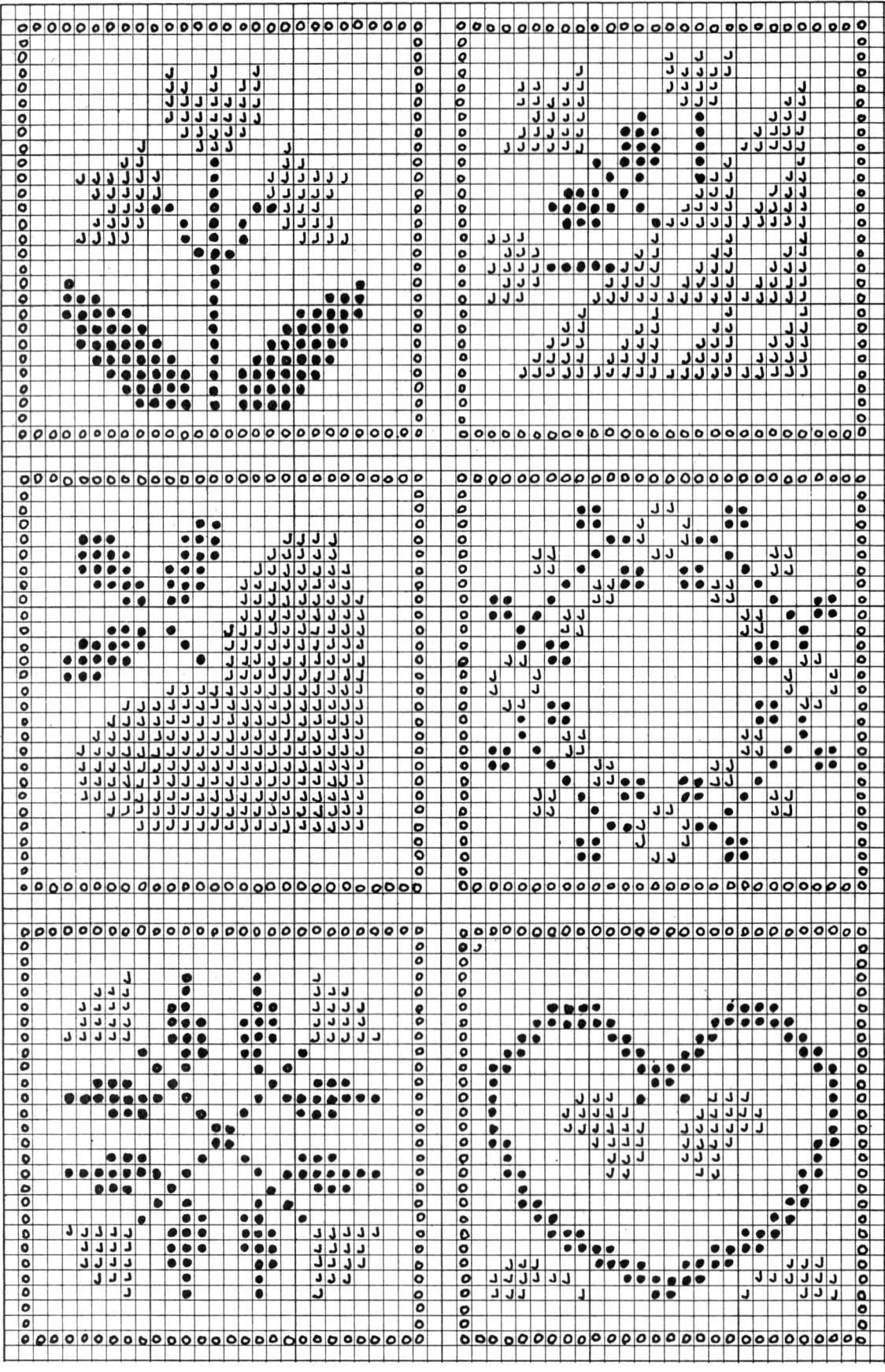

Floral Quilt

⏚ red		⊡ green
⊙ blue		— green backstitch

44

Allover Patterns

☒	dark pink
▨	gold
⬤	green

Gentle is the Breath of Spring Sampler

J	red	S	peach
O	blue	⊟	yellow
∴	light blue	●	green

Work letters in backstitch with red. Do not work straight lines between motifs.

46